Success in Key Stage Shakespeare

Scene-specific preparation for the 2007 national test

The Tempest

MICHAEL JONES
KEVIN DYKE
and GEORGHIA ELLINAS

www.harcourt.co.uk

✓ Free online support
✓ Useful weblinks
✓ 24 hour online ordering

01865 888058

Sam Deans   9Sh

From Harcourt

Introduction

Success in Key Stage 3 Shakespeare: **The Tempest** is designed to build on your teaching of the play as a whole and help you to improve the performance of all your students in the Key Stage 3 Shakespeare test. Together the *Success in Key Stage 3 Shakespeare:* **The Tempest** Student's Revision Book and the Teacher's Notes provide a revision programme and a schedule of 14 lessons, which ensure that students engage with and revise character, theme, language and performance in the context of the set extracts. Once you have worked through the activities with your students, they will have explored the set scenes according to the four key areas of test questioning and practised supporting these points with quotations from the set extracts.

The Teacher's Notes are available at www.heinemann.co.uk/literature. They include:
- a scheme of work for 14 revision lessons with lesson plans showing how the summary activities can be used to engage students and enhance understanding
- additional information to support the activities in the Student's Revision Book.

Using *Success in Key Stage 3 Shakespeare:* **The Tempest** to revise for the Key Stage 3 tests, means you can be secure in the knowledge that your students have been well prepared for the test and should feel confident about answering any question that may be asked.

Heinemann Educational Publishers
Halley Court, Jordan Hill, Oxford OX2 8EJ
Part of Harcourt Education

Heinemann is the registered trademark of Harcourt Education Limited

© Harcourt, 2006

First published 2006

10 09 08 07 06
10 9 8 7 6 5 4 3 2 1

British Library Cataloguing in Publication Data is available
from the British Library on request.

10-digit ISBN: 0 435 99718 1
13-digit ISBN: 978 0 435997 18 2

Designed by GD Associates
Typeset by 𝌆 Tek-Art, Croydon, Surrey

Original illustrations © Harcourt Education Limited, 2006
Illustrated by Andy Morris
Printed in the UK by Ashford Colour Press

Cover photo: © Corbis

Success in Key Stage 3 Shakespeare: *The Tempest*

Contents

The story of *The Tempest*

1 Alonso, King of Naples and Antonio the usurper Duke of Milan, with their followers, are shipwrecked on their way back from the marriage of Alonso's daughter.

2 Prospero tells his daughter Miranda how they were driven out from his Dukedom of Milan by his false brother Antonio and the King of Naples. Now, through his magical powers, Prospero has created the storm to right those wrongs.

3 Prospero checks what his spirit Ariel has done with the shipwrecked sailors, and then reminds Ariel of how he was rescued by Prospero from the witch Sycorax, mother of the creature Caliban.

4 Caliban, a monster-like creature, lusts after Miranda and resents Prospero for taking 'his' island from him.

5 Ferdinand, son of the King of Naples, follows Ariel's music until he meets Miranda. He is the first human she has met, and Prospero, when he realises that this is love at first sight, puts Ferdinand to the test.

6 Elsewhere on the island, the shipwrecked nobles, amazed at the freshness of their garments, wonder where they are, and lament the loss of Ferdinand.

7 Antonio encourages Sebastian to start plotting against Alonso, (as he had against Prospero) and they are stopped only by Ariel's magic.

8 Stephano and Trinculo, two of Alonso's shipwrecked servants, bump into Caliban, and introduce him to drink.

9 Ferdinand and Miranda fall in love, and Prospero accepts this.

10 Caliban encourages Stephano and Trinculo to kill Prospero.

11 Magical shapes, brought by Ariel, bring the evil men towards acknowledging their crimes, as Prospero planned.

12 Prospero gives Ferdinand Miranda's hand in marriage, and celebrates this with a magical pageant of goddesses who bless the couple.

13 Prospero remembers the conspiracy against him urged by Caliban, and uses Ariel's magic to distract and then torment the drunken three.

14 Prospero, now with all his enemies, past and present, in his power decides to forgive rather than to punish. He will give up the magic that has made possible the recognition and reconciliation that can now happen.

15 Prospero, having embraced Gonzalo, the one person who remained loyal to him, forgives Alonso and demands his dukedom back from his so-called brother, Antonio.

16 The innocence and purity of Ferdinand and Miranda signal a new beginning: the magic of the island has enabled the past crimes to be acknowledged and atoned for. Ariel's final task is to deal with Stephano, Trinculo and Caliban. Prospero no longer needs his magic, and we return from this on-stage island to the real world.

Set extracts – *The Tempest*

Extract 1: Act 1, Scene 2, lines 189 to 321

Character
Ariel's formal greeting shows Prospero's power

Language
The list of verbs emphasises how many things Ariel can do

ARIEL
All hail, great master! Grave sir, hail! I come
To answer thy best pleasure – be't to fly,   190
To swim, to dive into the fire, to ride
On the curled clouds. To thy strong biffing task
Ariel and all his quality.

PROSPERO
Hast thou, spirit,
Performed to point the tempest that I bade thee?

Theme
Prospero asks if Ariel has performed the tempest, showing how magic has been used

Performance
As he mentions each place, Ariel's voice and gestures should demonstrate his excitement

ARIEL
To every article.   195
I boarded the King's ship. Now on the beak,
Now in the waist, the deck, in every cabin,
I flamed amazement. Sometimes I'd divide,
And burn in many places. On the topmast,
The yards and bowsprit would I flame distinctly,   200
Then meet and join. Jove's lightnings, the precursors
O'the dreadful thunder-claps, more momentary
And sight-outrunning were not. The fire and cracks
Of sulphurous roaring the most mighty Neptune
Seemed to besiege, and make his bold waves tremble –   205
Yea, his dread trident shake.

Language
Jove and Neptune show how the storm frightened even the mythical gods

Character
Prospero shows how much he admires Ariel

PROSPERO
My brave spirit!
Who was so firm, so constant, that this coil
Would not infect his reason?

Theme
Disease and madness are affecting Prospero's enemies

ARIEL
Not a soul
But felt a fever of the mad, and played
Some tricks of desperation. All but mariners   210
Plunged in the foaming brine, and quit the vessel,
Then all afire with me. The King's son, Ferdinand,
With hair up-staring – then like reeds, not hair –
Was the first man that leaped; cried, 'Hell is empty,
And all the devils are here!'

Performance
As he says 'me', Ariel should stand tall and look proud of what he has done

Character
By asking for all the precise details Prospero shows how anxious he is that the storm has gone well

PROSPERO
Why, that's my spirit!   215
But was not this nigh shore?

ARIEL
Close by, my master.

Language
Ferdinand's cry shows how powerful the magic storm has been

Theme
Their clothes look as though they are brand new showing the illusion created by the magic

Theme
Prospero's magical power is apparent: he has selected only his enemies for treatment on the island

Language
The words 'charm' and 'dew' show how Ariel collects natural objects to make magic charms

Character
Ariel's description of the rest of the King's party going home shows how he can feel sadness even though he isn't human

Theme
There are many references to time, showing Prospero has to work quickly – he has only the time the play will last in which to work his magic

PROSPERO
But are they, Ariel, safe?

ARIEL
Not a hair perished:
On their sustaining garments not a blemish,
But fresher than before. And, as thou bad'st me,
In troops I have dispersed them 'bout the isle.   220
The King's son have I landed by himself –
Whom I left cooling of the air with sighs
In an odd angle of the isle, and sitting,
His arms in this sad knot. (*He folds his arms.*)

PROSPERO
Of the King's ship,
The mariners, say how thou hast disposed,   225
And all the rest o'the fleet.

ARIEL
Safely in the harbour
Is the King's ship. In the deep nook, where once
Thou call'dst me up at midnight to fetch dew
From the still-vexed Bermudas, there she's hid.
The mariners all under hatches stowed –   230
Who, with a charm joined to their suffered labour,
I have left asleep. And for the rest o'the fleet,
Which I dispersed, they all have met again,
And are upon the Mediterranean flote,
Bound sadly home for Naples –   235
Supposing that they saw the King's ship wrecked,
And his great person perish.

PROSPERO
Ariel, thy charge
Exactly is performed. But there's still more work.
What is the time o'the day?

ARIEL
Past the mid season.

PROSPERO
At least two glasses. The time 'twixt six and now   240
Must by us both be spent most preciously.

Performance
Ariel should show how Ferdinand looks by pretending to be him

Language
Words like 'safely', 'deep', 'stowed' and 'hid' emphasise how carefully Prospero has planned things so no one is hurt

ARIEL
Is there more toil? Since thou dost give me pains,
Let me remember thee what thou hast promised,
Which is not yet performed me.

PROSPERO
How now, moody? What is't thou canst demand?

ARIEL
My liberty.   245

PROSPERO
Before the time be out? No more!

ARIEL
I prithee,
Remember I have done thee worthy service;
Told thee no lies, made no mistakings, served
Without or grudge or grumblings. Thou did promise
To bate me a full year.

PROSPERO
Dost thou forget   250
From what a torment I did free thee?

ARIEL
No!

PROSPERO
Thou dost – and think'st it much to tread the ooze
Of the salt deep,
To run upon the sharp wind of the north,
To do me business in the veins o' the earth   255
When it is baked with frost.

ARIEL
I do not, sir.

PROSPERO
Thou liest, malignant thing! Hast thou forgot
The foul witch Sycorax, who with age and envy
Was grown into a hoop? Hast thou forgot her?

ARIEL
No, sir.

PROSPERO
Thou hast. Where was she born? Speak. Tell me!   260

ARIEL
Sir, in Algiers.

Performance

Prospero should use a sarcastic tone of voice to say this line

Theme

The evil black magic of Sycorax contrasts with Prospero's good 'white' magic

Character

The fierce rage that Sycorax showed to Ariel contrasts with Prospero's kinder character

Theme

The years that Ariel was imprisoned by Sycorax contrasts with the two days he still has to serve Prospero

Language

The powerful physical description should show how bad Ariel's suffering was

PROSPERO
O, was she so? I must
Once in a month recount what thou hast been,
Which thou forget'st. This damned witch Sycorax,
For mischiefs manifold, and sorceries terrible
To enter human hearing, from Algiers,   265
Thou know'st, was banished. For one thing she did
They would not take her life. Is not this true?

ARIEL
Ay, sir.

PROSPERO
This blue-eyed hag was hither brought with child,
And here was left by the sailors. Thou, my slave,   270
As thou report'st thyself, wast then her servant.
And, for thou wast a spirit too delicate
To act her earthly and abhorred commands,
Refusing her grand hests, she did confine thee,
By help of her more potent ministers,   275
And in her most unmitigable rage,
Into a cloven pine. Within which rift
Imprisoned thou didst painfully remain
A dozen years; within which space she died,
And left thee there – where thou didst vent thy groans 280
As fast as mill-wheels strike. Then was this island –
Save for the son that she did litter here,
A freckled whelp hag-born – not honoured with
A human shape.

ARIEL
Yes, Caliban her son.

PROSPERO
Dull thing, I say so: he, that Caliban,   285
Whom now I keep in service. Thou best know'st
What torment I did find thee in. Thy groans
Did make wolves howl, and penetrate the breasts
Of ever-angry bears. It was torment
To lay upon the damned, which Sycorax   290
Could not again undo. It was mine Art,
When I arrived and heard thee, that made gape
The pine, and let thee out.

Language

All the negative words like 'damned', 'terrible' and 'hag' are used by Prospero to show Sycorax is evil and to show how good he is in contrast

Theme

The terrible revenge Sycorax took against Ariel contrasts with the forgiveness Prospero will show to his enemies

Theme

Prospero's good magic was able to defeat the evil spell Sycorax had used

Character

All the reminders of how badly he was treated by Sycorax make Ariel realise he is fortunate, so he will behave

Performance

Ariel should show how pleased he is that Prospero's criticism has finished by suddenly becoming livelier

Language

Prospero's gentle words to Miranda contrast with the angry language he used to Ariel and show how much he cares for his daughter

Theme

Although Prospero has power over Caliban 'his slave', Caliban also has power because Prospero depends on him as well

Performance

The exclamation marks show Prospero should shout harshly

ARIEL
I thank thee, master.

PROSPERO
If thou more murmur'st, I will rend an oak,
And peg thee in his knotty entrails, till   295
Thou hast howled away twelve winters.

ARIEL
Pardon, master.
I will be correspondent to command,
And do my spiriting gently.

PROSPERO
Do so!
And after two days I will discharge thee.

ARIEL
That's my noble master! What shall I do?   300
Say what? What shall I do?

PROSPERO
Go make thyself
Like a nymph o'the sea. Be subject to
No sight but thine and mine: invisible
To every eyeball else. Go take this shape,
And hither come in't. Go! Hence, with diligence!   305

Exit ARIEL.

(To MIRANDA) Awake, dear heart, awake! Thou hast
Slept well.
Awake!

MIRANDA
The strangeness of your story put
Heaviness in me.

PROSPERO
Shake it off. Come on:
We'll visit Caliban my slave, who never
Yields us kind answer.

MIRANDA
'Tis a villain, sir,   310
I do not love to look on.

PROSPERO
But as 'tis,
We cannot miss him. He does make our fire,
Fetch in our wood, and serves in offices
That profit us. What, ho! Slave! Caliban!
Thou earth, thou: speak!

Character

Prospero's threat emphasises that he can be a tyrant

Theme

The precise time of two days contrasts with the years Ariel was imprisoned by Sycorax

Performance

As she wakes from her deep sleep, Miranda should move slowly and sleepily in contrast with Ariel's lively actions

Language

The repeated word 'slave' emphasises Prospero's power over Caliban

CALIBAN (*Calling from the far side of Prospero's cave*)
There's wood enough within!   315

PROSPERO
Come forth, I say! There's other business for thee.
Come, thou tortoise! When?

Enter ARIEL, like a water-nymph.

Fine apparition! My quaint Ariel,
Hark in thine ear. (*He whispers instructions to* ARIEL.)

ARIEL
My lord, it shall be done.

Exit.

PROSPERO
Thou poisonous slave, got by the devil himself   320
Upon thy wicked dam, come forth!

Extract 2: Act 5, Scene 1, lines 1 to 134

In front of Prospero's cave.
Enter PROSPERO in his magic cloak, and ARIEL.

PROSPERO
Now does my project gather to a head.
My charms crack not, my spirits obey; and time
Goes upright with his carriage. How's the day?

ARIEL
On the sixth hour – at which time, my lord,
You said our work should cease.

PROSPERO
I did say so,   5
When first I raised the tempest. Say, my spirit,
How fares the King and's followers?

ARIEL
Confined together
In the same fashion as you gave in charge,
Just as you left them: all prisoners, sir,
In the lime-grove which weather-fends your cell.   10
They cannot budge till your release. The King,
His brother, and yours, abide all three distracted,
And the remainder mourning over them,
Brimful of sorrow and dismay – but chiefly
Him you termed, sir, 'The good old lord, Gonzalo'.   15
His tears run down his beard, like winter's drops
From eaves of reeds. Your charm so strongly works 'em,
That if you now beheld them, your affections
Would become tender.

PROSPERO
Dost thou think so, spirit?

ARIEL
Mine would, sir, were I human.

PROSPERO
And mine shall.   20
Hast thou, which art but air, a touch, a feeling
Of their afflictions, and shall not myself –
One of their kind, that relish all as sharply
Passion as they – be kindlier moved than thou art?
Though with their high wrongs I am struck to the quick, 25
Yet with my nobler reason 'gainst my fury
Do I take part. The rarer action is
In virtue than in vengeance. They being penitent,
The sole drift of my purpose doth extend
Not a frown further. Go release them, Ariel.   30
My charms I'll break, their senses I'll restore,
And they shall be themselves.

Language
The word 'project' reminds the audience that all that has happened is part of Prospero's plan

Character
Ariel shows how determined he is that Prospero remembers his promise

Language
The powerful image of Gonzalo's tears shows how much Ariel has been affected by what he has seen

Performance
As he remembers his enemies' bad treatment of him, Prospero should look angry and speak angrily; then he should speak and look more gently as he thinks of forgiveness

Theme
Not only will they wake from the magic spell but also they will become their true selves

Theme
The references to time reinforce the importance of time for Prospero's plan

Performance
As he says this speech, Ariel should show through his movements how the characters appear while imprisoned by the magic

Character
Ariel's words have made Prospero decide to forgive his enemies, contrasting with his anger in Extract 1

Language
The words 'touch', 'feeling', 'relish' and 'sharply' all refer to emotional feelings and emphasise how Prospero has been affected

Theme
At this point the theme of forgiveness and vengeance is shown in the choice Prospero makes

ARIEL
I'll fetch them, sir.

Exit.

PROSPERO
Ye elves of hills, brooks, standing lakes, and groves;
And ye that on the sands with printless foot
Do chase the ebbing Neptune, and do fly him 35
When he comes back; you demi-puppets that
By moonshine do the green sour ringlets make,
Whereof the ewe not bites; and you whose pastime
Is to make midnight mushrooms, that rejoice
To hear the solemn curfew – by whose aid 40
(Weak masters though ye be) I have bedimmed
The noontide sun, called forth the mutinous winds,
And 'twixt the green sea and the azured vault
Set roaring war. To the dread rattling thunder
Have I given fire, and rifted Jove's stout oak 45
With his own bolt. The strong-based promontory
Have I made shake, and by the spurs plucked up
The pine and cedar. Graves at my command
Have waked their sleepers, oped, and let 'em forth
By my so potent Art. But this rough magic 50
I here abjure. And, when I have required
Some heavenly music (which even now I do),
To work mine end upon their senses that
This airy charm is for, I'll break my staff,
Bury it certain fathoms in the earth, 55
And deeper than did ever plummet sound
I'll drown my book.

Solemn music plays.

PROSPERO *marks a magic circle on the ground.*

Re-enter ARIEL. *King* ALONSO *follows, moving as if driven
mad, with* GONZALO *tending to him.* SEBASTIAN *and*
ANTONIO *follow, also appearing maddened, accompanied
by* ADRIAN *and* FRANCISCO. *All enter* PROSPERO'S
magic circle and stand there, still, under the power of his spell.
PROSPERO *watches them, then speaks.*

A solemn air, and the best comforter
To an unsettled fancy, cure thy brains,
Now useless, boiled within thy skull! There stand, 60
For you are spell-stopped.
Holy Gonzalo, honourable man,
Mine eyes, ev'n sociable to the show of thine,

Performance
Prospero should show his power by standing proudly and point towards different places as he mentions each of the magic creatures

Character
The repetition of 'I' emphasises Prospero's pride in his power and how hard it is for him to give it up

Language
The short sentence after all the descriptions of the magic powers emphasises that this is the moment of decision when he finally gives up his powers

Character
Prospero's serious decision is made clear by the heavy sound of the words 'deeper', 'plummet' and 'drown'

Performance
As they come onto the stage Alonso, Antonio and Sebastian should hold their hands to their heads showing the power of the magic spell

Theme
The word 'cure' shows that power is going to be used for good

Language
The lists of places ('hills', 'brooks') and the different creatures ('elves', 'demi-puppets') emphasise how far his magic power spreads

Theme
The dangerous power of magic is emphasised by the references to night

Theme
The list of magic powers builds up to opening graves and shows the great power he is going to give up

Performance
As he says these final words Prospero should speak slowly and seriously, holding the staff and the book towards the audience

Language
The words 'cure' and 'comforter' make it clear that Prospero is now going to stop punishing them

Character
Prospero's affection for Gonzalo, who helped him escape with Miranda, is clear when he starts to cry

Theme
Goodness will win over evil in Alonso, Sebastian and Antonio as a result of Prospero's magic

Performance
As he looks at each person caught in the magic power Prospero should show his different feelings: kind to Gonzalo but bitter to the others

Performance
As he looks at them under the spell he should sound thoughtful, then suddenly become lively as he decides to show himself as the duke

Character
Ariel's happiness contrasts with his anger in Extract 1

Performance
Ariel's movements should be lively to show how happy he is

Performance
Ariel should move swiftly as he says these words

Fall fellowly drops. The charm dissolves apace –
And as the morning steals upon the night,
Melting the darkness, so their rising senses
Begin to chase the ignorant fumes that mantle
Their clearer reason. O good Gonzalo, 65
My true preserver, and a loyal sir
To him thou follow'st! I will pay thy graces
Home both in word and deed. Most cruelly 70
Didst thou, Alonso, use me and my daughter.
Thy brother was a furtherer in the act.
Thou art pinched for't now, Sebastian! Flesh and blood,
You, brother mine, that entertained ambition, 75
Expelled remorse and nature – whom, with Sebastian,
Whose inward pinches therefore are most strong,
Would here have killed your King – I do forgive thee,
Unnatural though thou art! Their understanding
Begins to swell – and the approaching tide 80
Will shortly fill the reasonable shore,
That now lies foul and muddy. Not one of them
That yet looks on me, or would know me. Ariel,
Fetch me the hat and rapier in my cell.

Exit ARIEL.

I will discase me, and myself present 85
As I was sometime Milan. Quickly, Spirit!
Thou shalt ere long be free.

*Re-enter ARIEL, with hat and rapier. As he helps to dress
PROSPERO, and remove his magic cloak, he sings.*

ARIEL
Where the bee sucks, there suck I.
In a cowslip's bell I lie.
There I couch when owls do cry. 90
On the bat's back I do fly –
After summer merrily.
Merrily, merrily shall I live now
Under the blossom that hangs on the bough!

PROSPERO
Why, that's my dainty Ariel! I shall miss thee – 95
But yet thou shalt have freedom. So, so, so.
To the King's ship, invisible as thou art.
There shalt thou find the mariners asleep
Under the hatches. The master and the boatswain
Being awake, enforce them to this place, 100
And presently, I prithee.

ARIEL
I drink the air before me, and return
Or ere your pulse twice beat.

Exit.

Language
The contrast between 'night' and 'morning' and between 'ignorant' and 'reason' shows that good will come of the magic Prospero has used

Character
Prospero forgives his evil brother but the audience sees how hard it is for him to forgive

Language
The contrast between the clear water of the tide that will cover the 'foul and muddy' shore shows goodness defeating evil and disease

Language
The natural images show Ariel will live a free life like a bird; the repetition of 'merrily' emphasises his happiness

Theme
Ariel's joyful song reinforces the theme of goodness defeating evil

Character
Prospero shows how much he will miss Ariel

Theme
The careful planning of the magic is emphasised

GONZALO
All torment, trouble, wonder and amazement
Inhabits here. Some heavenly power guide us   105
Out of this fearful country!

PROSPERO
Behold, sir King,
The wronged Duke of Milan, Prospero.
For more assurance that a living prince
Does now speak to thee, I embrace thy body –
(*Embraces* ALONSO)
And to thee and thy company I bid   110
A hearty welcome.

ALONSO
Whether thou be'st he or no,
Or some enchanted trifle to abuse me,
As late I have been, I not know. Thy pulse
Beats, as of flesh and blood – and, since I saw thee,
The affliction of my mind amends, with which,   115
I fear, a madness held me. This must crave –
An if this be at all – a most strange story.
Thy dukedom I resign, and do entreat
Thou pardon me my wrongs. But how should Prospero
Be living and be here?

PROSPERO (*To* GONZALO)
First, noble friend,
Let me embrace thine age, whose honour cannot   120
Be measured or confined. (*Embraces him*)

GONZALO
Whether this be
Or be not, I'll not swear!

PROSPERO
You do yet taste
Some subtleties o'the isle, that will not let you
Believe things certain. Welcome, my friends all!   125

Theme

Prospero's power cannot succeed in changing Sebastian and Antonio but he can control them through threats

Theme

This is the climax of the themes of good, evil and revenge when the audience sees whether Prospero will be able to forgive his brother

Character

Prospero shows his strong belief in forgiveness by forgiving Antonio

(*Aside to* SEBASTIAN *and* ANTONIO) But you, my brace of lords, were I so minded,
I here could pluck his highness' frown upon you,
And justify you traitors, at this time
I will tell no tales.

SEBASTIAN
(*Aside*) The devil speaks in him!

PROSPERO
No.
(*To* ANTONIO) For you, most wicked sir, whom to call brother   130
Would even infect my mouth, I do forgive
Thy rankest fault – all of them – and require
My dukedom of thee: which perforce, I know,
Thou must restore.

Performance

As he speaks to Antonio, Prospero should stand close to him and look at him directly

Language

The words 'wicked' and 'infect my mouth' show how bitter Prospero is and how hard it is to forgive his brother

Character grid

Working with a partner, think and talk about the statements in the first column. Then fill in your responses in the appropriate column, giving evidence from the set extracts. Explain and explore your thinking. The first line has been completed for you as an example.

Prospero Statement	Response	Yes/No	Evidence	Explanation	Exploration
Prospero is a cruel master to Ariel.	Definitely. Yes, on balance. Not really. No way.	Yes.	'My brave spirit!' (Prospero, Act 1, Scene 2, line 207) 'How now moody?' (Prospero, Act 1, Scene 2, line 244) 'I will rend an oak, and peg thee in his knotty entrails' (Prospero, Act 1, Scene 2, line 295). 'yet thou shalt have freedom' (Prospero, Act 5, Scene 1, line 96)	Ariel does everything Prospero asks of him. Prospero did release Ariel from the cloven pine, and although he is angered in Extract 1 when Ariel reminds him of the promise of freedom, he does finally release his 'dainty Ariel' at the end of the play.	Prospero threatens to torment Ariel just as Sycorax did. This makes us question the nature of his magic and his self-control in Extract 1 because he seems unreasonable. In Extract 2 we see how much more self-knowledge and self-control he has developed.
Prospero loves Miranda but is a harsh father to her.	Definitely. Yes, on balance. Not really. No way.				
Prospero's magic is more important in Extract 1 than in Extract 2.	Definitely. Yes, on balance. Not really. No way.				
Prospero's anger in Extract 1 makes his control more impressive in Extract 2.	Definitely. Yes, on balance. Not really. No way.				
The audience will think that Prospero is wrong to keep quiet about the plotting of Antonio and Sebastian.	Definitely. Yes, on balance. Not really. No way.				
Prospero develops more than any other character in the short time between these two extracts.	Definitely. Yes, on balance. Not really. No way.				
These extracts show us Prospero the man, more than Prospero the magician.	Definitely. Yes, on balance. Not really. No way.				

Focus on character

Highlight the key words in the tables below and fill in the blank rows with your own points, quotations and personal responses.

Extract 1: Act 1, Scene 2, lines 189 to 321

Points	Quotations	Personal responses
Ariel has a great deal of energy and enjoys his powers.	Ariel: ' … be't to fly, / To swim, to dive into the fire, to ride / On the curled clouds' (Act 1, Scene 2, lines 190–92).	This energy comes from the strong verbs Ariel uses to describe how he works for Prospero. The image of him riding the 'curled cloud' as if he was riding a wild horse is very effective.
Ariel is reliable and carefully follows Prospero's instructions. He resents it when Prospero continues to give him work and does not keep his promise to free him.	Ariel: 'I have done thee worthy service; / Told thee no lies, made no mistakings, served / Without grudge or grumblings' (Act 1, Scene 2, lines 248–9).	Ariel feels he has earned his freedom because he has been such a dutiful servant.
Prospero does not like his authority to be questioned.	Prospero: 'How now, moody? / What is't thou canst demand?' (Act 1, Scene 2, line 244).	These terse questions show Prospero is angry with Ariel. By calling him moody, he suggests it is Ariel who is unreasonable.
Prospero is prepared to be ruthless to get his own way.	Prospero: 'If thou more murmur'st, I will rend an oak, / And peg thee in his knotty entrails, till / Thou has howled away twelve winters' (Act 1, Scene 2, lines 294–6).	Prospero's punishment for Ariel is harsh, given Ariel's request. The word 'howled' emphasises how Ariel would suffer.

Extract 2: Act 5, Scene 1, lines 1 to 134

Points	Quotations	Personal responses
Ariel senses how much the humans have suffered and feels it is time they were forgiven.	Ariel: 'Your charm so strongly works 'em, / That if you now beheld them, your affections / Would become tender' (Act 5, Scene 1, lines 17–18).	Unlike Prospero, Ariel has witnessed the suffering that Prospero's magic has had on the King, his followers and Gonzalo.
Prospero believes he has moral and intellectual superiority.	Prospero: 'Though with their high wrongs I am struck to the quick, / Yet with my nobler reason 'gainst my fury / Do I take part' (Act 5, Scene 1, lines 25–6).	Prospero shows he can control his emotions and forgive his enemies by using his reason. This makes him a better man.
Prospero has enjoyed the power he has had over the natural world.	Prospero: 'Graves at my command / Have waked their sleepers, oped, and let 'em forth / By my so potent Art' (Act 5, Scene 1, lines 48–50).	Waking the dead is a frightening power. The audience would be horrified, as only God should raise the dead.
Prospero makes sure Sebastian and Antonio know he is still watching them.	Prospero: 'But you, my brace of lords, were I so minded, / I here could pluck his highness' frown upon you, / And justify you traitors. At this time / I will tell no tales' (Act 5, Scene 1, lines 126–8).	Prospero has not completely relinquished his power, as he can still expose Sebastian and Antonio's plot to kill the King.

Focus on theme

Highlight the key words in the following tables and fill in the blank rows with your own points, quotations and personal responses.

Extract 1: Act 1, Scene 2, lines 189 to 321

Points	Quotations	Personal responses
Freedom and control		
The promise of his freedom has made Ariel eager to finish his duties. When Ariel questions Prospero about his freedom, praise turns to indignation.	Ariel: 'great master', 'strong bidding' (Act 1, Scene 2, lines 189 and 192); 'Is there more toil?' (Act 1, Scene 2, line 242). Prospero: 'Hast thou, spirit, / Performed to point the tempest that I bade thee?' (Act 1, Scene 2, line 193); 'My brave spirit! (Act 1, Scene 2, line 206).	Despite Ariel's magical powers, he is a servant to a human being who treats him harshly. The idea of freedom and control comes early in the play.
Prospero is conscious of his power over Ariel, and of time that is passing on the island (and in the theatre). He maintains his control by reminding Ariel of his former suffering inflicted by 'the foul witch Sycorax'.	Prospero: 'How now moody? (Act 1, Scene 2, line 244); 'Before the time be out?' (Act 1, Scene 2, line246); Dost thou forget / From what a torment I did free thee?' (Act 1, Scene 2, line 250); 'Thou liest, malignant thing!' (Act 1, Scene 2, line 257); 'If thou more murmur'st, I will rend an oak, / And peg thee in his knotty entrails' (Act 1, Scene 2, lines 294–5).	Prospero's anger ignites very quickly and hardly seems justified in the light of Ariel's recent magical efforts. We may think this mad magician is like the witch he describes.
Real and magical		
We learn that the tempest was magical and the mariners are all 'safe'. Prospero's magical power has some of the strangeness of discoveries made in Shakespeare's time. Exploration was dangerous.	Ariel: 'Now on the beak, / Now in the waist, the deck, in every cabin, / I flamed amazement' (Act 1, Scene 2, lines 195–7); 'Not a hair perished: / On their sustaining garments not a blemish' (Act 1, Scene 2, lines 219–20); 'Thou call'dst me up at midnight to fetch dew / From the still-vexed Bermudas' (Act 1, Scene 2, line 229); '... the rest o' the fleet, / ... Bound sadly home for Naples – / Supposing that they saw the King's ship wrecked' (Act 1, Scene 2, lines 233–5).	We are being moved out of the normal world into an island of magic and mystery. Prospero's enemies have been removed from the real world to a magical island of imagination – like the theatre. Shakespeare's audience would have heard of voyages to strange lands such as the Bermudas.
Prospero's reminder to Ariel makes us aware of the power of his magic but also of the quickness of his anger.	Prospero: 'It was mine Art, / ... that made gape / The pine and let thee out' (Act 1, Scene 2, lines 291–2).	Prospero's magic proved stronger than that of Sycorax, but magic seems to have potential for good or evil.
Vengeance and forgiveness		
Prospero is already using the magic of the island to test out the courage and sanity of his enemies.	Prospero: 'Who was so firm, so constant, that this coil / Would not infect his reason?' (Act 1, Scene 2, line 206).	Prospero is excited at the outcome of his magical tempest test. This makes us curious.
Prospero wants his shipwrecked enemies safe, when he could have had them killed. He has a clear plan in mind, and his timing matches the length of the play.	Prospero: 'But are they, Ariel, safe?' (Act 1, Scene 2, line 217); 'The time 'twixt six and now / Must by us both be spent most preciously' (Act 1, Scene 2, line 240).	We realise that Prospero has a definite purpose, and we assume that revenge is part of it.

Extract 2: Act 5, Scene 1, lines 1 to 134

Points	Quotations	Personal responses
Freedom and control		
The time is almost up: characters (and the audience) must leave the imagined world of the play for 'real' life. Antonio is not repentant but is still not punished as we might have expected.	Prospero: '… you are spell-stopped' (Act 5, Scene 1, line 61); 'Their understanding / Begins to swell' (Act 5, Scene 1, lines 79–80); '[I] require / My dukedom of thee: which perforce, I know, / Thou must restore' (Act 5, Scene 1, lines 132–4).	The magical control that gave Prospero power over his enemies is outside the real world; they are returning to normality and to self-knowledge. Prospero's control here is moral rather than magical
Ariel has been the sign of Prospero's magical power: freeing him removes Prospero's control over him.	Prospero: 'Quickly Spirit! / Thou shalt 'ere long be free' (Act 5, Scene 1, line 86).	Prospero no longer needs the magic that Ariel represents, and no longer needs to have power over Ariel.
Real and magical		
Prospero's resumption of his Milanese clothing symbolises the return to normal living.	Prospero: 'By my so potent Art. But this rough magic / I here abjure … / … I'll break my staff, / Bury it certain fathoms in the earth, / And deeper than did ever plummet sound / I'll drown my book (Act 5 Scene 1, lines 50–56); 'I will discase me, and myself present / As I was sometime in Milan' (Act 5, Scene 1, line 85).	For Prospero to truly triumph over his enemies, and over himself, he needs to do so without his magic. The physical changing of cloaks tells us that the magic has done its work and is no longer needed.
The shipwrecked characters do not understand what has happened to them; they are still disorientated.	Gonzalo: 'All torment, trouble, wonder and amazement / Inhabits here' (Act 5, Scene 1, lines 104–5).	Gonzalo, the only person loyal to Prospero, is the first to regain his senses, but is bewildered by what has happened.
Vengeance and forgiveness		
Prospero's plans are coming to fruition; he has been in control of his 'project' from the start of the play.	Prospero: 'Now does my project gather to a head. / My charms crack not, my spirits obey; and time / Goes upright in his carriage (Act 5, Scene 1, lines 1–3).	We recognise that Prospero (like Shakespeare) has been in control for the length of the play.
Non-human Ariel suggests forgiveness rather than the vengeance the original crimes would justify.	Ariel: 'That if you now beheld them, your affections / Would become tender' (Act 5, Scene 1, line 18); 'Mine would, sir, were I human' (Act 5, Scene 1, line 19).	The choice between revenge and forgiveness is made very clear by Ariel.
Prospero's decision to forgive is a difficult one for him, but shows his new power over his own feelings.	Prospero: 'Though with their high wrongs I am struck to the quick, / Yet with my nobler reason 'gainst my fury / Do I take part' (Act 5, Scene 1, lines 25–6).	The power of magic means that the real battle has been within Prospero, rather than between him and his enemies.
The self-knowledge Prospero shows here is hard won, but convincing to an audience.	Prospero: 'The rarer action is / in virtue than in vengeance. They being penitent, / The sole drift of my purpose doth extend / Not a frown further (Act 5, Scene 1, lines 26–30).	We admire the magical artistry Prospero used has to bring recognition to others as well as himself.
Prospero forgives those who have wronged him, even though his memory of their crimes is fresh.	Prospero: 'I do forgive thee, / Unnatural though thou art!' (Act 5, Scene 1, line 79); 'I do forgive / Thy rankest fault' (Act 5, Scene 1, line 131).	This forgiveness shows Prospero's victory over himself and over his desire for revenge.

Focus on language

Highlight the key words in the tables below. Fill in the blank rows with examples of uses of language that you think have a significant impact on an audience.

Extract 1: Act 1, Scene 2, lines 189 to 321

Points	Quotations	Personal responses
Prospero likes complete obedience from his servants. When Ariel wants his freedom Prospero's language becomes nasty.	Prospero: 'Thou liest, malignant thing!' (Act 1, Scene 2, line 257).	He accuses Ariel unjustly. The word 'malignant' has hard g and t sounds. The word 'thing' shows no respect for his hard-working servant.
Prospero calls Sycorax a 'damned witch', but then threatens Ariel with a worse torture if he complains.	Prospero: 'I will rend an oak, / And peg thee in his knotty entrails' (Act 1, Scene 2, lines 294–5).	Ironically, Prospero is as cruel as Sycorax. His words sound violent.
Prospero treats Caliban as a slave because he tried to rape Miranda. He has taken Caliban's island from him.	Prospero: ' … serves in offices / That profit us' (Act 1, Scene 2, lines 313–14).	Prospero is master of the island, and he calls both Ariel and Caliban 'slaves'. He threatens to torture them if necessary.

Extract 2: Act 5, Scene 1, lines 1 to 134

Points	Quotations	Personal responses
Prospero learns from Ariel who responds to Gonzalo's tears even though he is a spirit.	Prospero: 'a touch, a feeling / Of their afflictions' (Act 5, Scene 1, line 21).	Prospero the magician suddenly speaks of human feelings.
Prospero speaks a spell to the elves with natural, airy words. He has made them obey him.	Prospero: 'mutinous winds'; 'roaring war'; 'dread rattling thunder' (Act 5, Scene 1, lines 42–4).	These violent words show how Prospero knows he has abused the natural freedom of Nature with his 'potent Art'.
Prospero struggles with anger as he tries to show mercy. He calls Gonzalo 'good' but turns angrily on Alonso.	Prospero: 'Most cruelly / Didst thou, Alonso, use me and my daughter' (Act 5, Scene 1, line 71).	He speaks angrily but he still forgives them. He knows that Sebastian and Antonio are 'traitors' but keeps quiet.

Focus on performance

Highlight the key words in the tables below and fill in the blank rows with your own points, quotations and personal responses.

Extract 1: Act 1, Scene 2, lines 189 to 321

Points	Quotations	Personal responses
In his performance, the actor playing Ariel shows he understands the feelings of the humans he sees.	Ariel: ' … and sitting, / His arms in this sad knot' (Act 1, Scene 2, lines 224–5).	The actor folds his arms like Ferdinand, helping us to 'see' Ferdinand's sadness as he thinks his father is dead.
The actor playing Ariel shows how quickly he becomes meek and obedient when Prospero is angry with him.	Ariel: 'Pardon, master. / I will be correspondent to command, / And do my spiriting gently' (Act 1, Scene 2, lines 297–8).	By behaving so politely and looking sad, the actor shows us how much Prospero's criticism has affected Ariel.
The powerful anger Prospero feels towards Ariel should be clear from the actor's performance.	Prospero: 'Thou liest, malignant thing!' (Act 1, Scene 2, line 257).	Through Prospero's voice and gestures we realise Ariel seems to have forgotten he was rescued by him.
The contrast between Prospero's love for Miranda and hatred of Caliban should be clear.	Prospero: 'Awake, dear heart, awake!' (Act 1, Scene 2, line 306); 'Thou poisonous slave, got by the devil himself' (Act 1, Scene 2, line 320).	The actor shows us why Prospero hates Caliban by speaking angrily to him and gently to Miranda.

Extract 2: Act 5, Scene 1, lines 1 to 134

Points	Quotations	Personal responses
The actor playing Ariel shows how other characters such as the King and Gonzalo are suffering.	Ariel: 'His tears run down his beard, like winter's drops / From eaves of reeds' (Act 5, Scene 1, line 16).	Through description and gesture, the actor should make us feel the suffering of the people affected by the magic.
The moment Prospero decides to give up his magic power should be made clear by the actor.	Prospero: 'I'll break my staff, / Bury it certain fathoms in the earth' (Act 5, Scene 1, lines 54–5).	The actor should speak slowly to make us see this great moment of decision.
The different feelings Prospero has towards the different members of the King's party should be clear.	Prospero: 'Let me embrace thine age' (Act 5, Scene 1, line 120); 'For you, most wicked sir, whom to call brother / Would even infect my mouth' (Act 5, Scene 1, line 130).	We see the way Prospero feels towards each person by what he says to each person.
The joy of Ariel's freedom should be shown by the actor.	Ariel: 'Merrily, merrily shall I live now' (Act 5, Scene 1, line 94).	We should see how much Ariel will enjoy his freedom when it comes.

The Key Stage 3 Shakespeare test

How to approach the test

Remember that:

- The Shakespeare test accounts for 18 out of the 50 marks for reading. You gain marks by showing you understand and have responded to Shakespeare.
- The way you write matters because it enables you to make your points effectively, but you will not be judged on how well you write. No marks are given (or taken off) for spelling or expression.
- The extracts you must write about will be printed in the test paper. Don't make the mistake of writing about all the set scenes – concentrate on those two extracts.
- PQR (**P**oint, **Q**uotation, **R**esponse) is better than PEE (**P**oint, **E**xplanation, **E**xample) because it includes your personal reaction to the play.
- Short quotations are better than long ones because they save you time in the test.

And, by the way …
since you will have to write about both extracts, you are not likely to be asked to focus on characters like Gonzalo, who doesn't appear at all in Extract 1, or Miranda who doesn't appear in Extract 2.

Revision
You can use this book to help with your preparation for the test by:
- looking back at the illustrated outline of the play on pages 4 and 5 to remind yourself of the sequence of events
- making sure that you are familiar with the quotations by and about Prospero and Ariel, and that you are used to telling other people your thoughts about them
- getting your head round the four 'big ideas' of character, language, themes and performance by talking with others about the points and quotations on pages 18–22
- planning answers to some or all of the sample questions on page 25
- working out the strengths (and there are many) of the sample answer, and what could be done to improve it
- looking at the marking criteria on page 24 enough to understand why marks are awarded by the examiners, and making sure that you can do what is needed.

What do I need to remember about how the Shakespeare paper will be marked?
Your understanding of *The Tempest* is assessed only for reading.
- No marks are given (or taken off) for spelling or expression, but the way you write does matter because it enables you to make your points effectively.
- You are not expected to write about the play as a whole, but to refer to the extracts given on the test paper. These extracts will be taken from the set scenes which are on pages 6 to 16 of this book.

Key Stage 3 marking

What will the question be on?

The question on *The Tempest* should be on **one** of the areas (or 'big ideas') below, although you can refer to the other areas as part of your answer:

- why characters behave as they do in the extracts given
- the impact of the language used in the extracts
- ideas, themes and issues that are relevant to the extracts
- how these extracts might be performed in the theatre.

How will my answer be marked?

The emphasis in marking will depend on the focus of the question, but generally answers are awarded level 5 or above if they:

- include comment on both of the extracts given on the paper
- reveal some understanding of character and dramatic action
- refer to the main features of the language in the extracts and the effect it might have
- show some awareness of how an audience might respond
- illustrate points made by picking out words or phrases from the text as evidence
- include your personal response to specific aspects of the extracts.

What are the different mark bands?

Working with a partner, look at the table below. It gives you the examiner's reasons for putting answers to a question about language in *The Tempest* in different mark bands. Then read the sample answer on page 26 and the suggestions for improving it. Discuss what else could be done to earn a higher band for the sample essay.

Band	Marking criteria
1	Mainly retelling the story, but a few facts and opinions with a quotation will still only reach this band.
2	A little explanation and some broad references to the text, e.g. Prospero is angry with Ariel, so he calls him 'moody'. This answer may not relate very closely to the question.
3	General understanding of the question. Prospero likes his own way so he calls Ariel 'moody' when he asks for his freedom. This shows some limited awareness of language as you are linking 'moody' to Prospero's character.
4	Some discussion. This is a very hard band to achieve unless you give a personal response to the question, e.g. I think Prospero is a bully because he wants his own way and abuses his servant Ariel when he asks for his freedom by calling him 'moody'. Here you are showing the effects of language by linking Prospero's words with the way he treats his servant. It is the sort of answer you would give in class, but now you have to write your opinion down with support from the text.
5	Clear focus on the essay title. You not only have to make a comment, with support from the text, but you have to show how the language works. You would still say Prospero is a bully who wants all his orders carried out 'to point', but you should explore Prospero's reaction in his language. 'Malignant thing' would be better to use because the language is more violent. There is a long, hard word followed by 'thing' which shows contempt and disgust. The words sound nasty.
6	For this band you have to show clear understanding of the question on language, character, theme or performance and show analysis. You have to explore why Prospero is a bully; he is sole ruler and can do what he likes. He treats all the other inhabitants of the island he has taken over as servants or, in Caliban's case, a slave. They have to do as he says 'to point' (embedded quote). Ariel is not allowed to ask for freedom from 'toil' (embedded quote) even though he has served Prospero well by bringing his enemies to the island. It is obvious that Ariel does not want this work, but Prospero's language shows that he will not listen; he can only bully. The 'delicate' Ariel is called 'malignant thing'. Prospero spits the harsh *g* and *t* sounds out as he calls him evil. A 'thing' is worthless and was a harsh term of abuse in Shakespeare's day. This is hardly the behaviour of a good ruler.

Sample questions

Themes
- Power and control
- Reality and magic
- Vengeance and forgiveness

- How do these two extracts show Prospero's use of magical power to control events in the play?
- How are the ideas of freedom and imprisonment shown in these two extracts?
- How far do these two extracts suggest that forgiveness is a greater victory than vengeance?

Language
1. How is language used in these two extracts to show different aspects of Prospero's power?
2. What does Prospero's use of language in these two extracts show about his feelings towards the other characters?

Character
1. Explain how these two extracts show how Prospero controls events in the play.
2. How do these two extracts show the relationship between Prospero and Ariel?
3. How do these two extracts show changes in Prospero's attitudes to other characters?

Performance
1. What advice would you give to the actor playing Prospero on how to convey the change in his attitudes to his enemies?
2. If you were directing *The Tempest* what advice would you give to the actor playing Ariel on how to convey his different moods?

Unpacking the question: an example

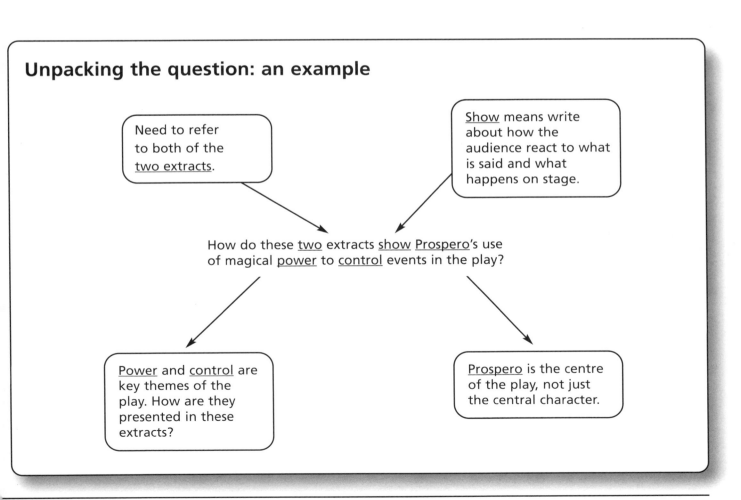

Need to refer to both of the <u>two extracts</u>.

<u>Show</u> means write about how the audience react to what is said and what happens on stage.

How do these <u>two</u> extracts <u>show</u> <u>Prospero</u>'s use of magical <u>power</u> to <u>control</u> events in the play?

<u>Power</u> and <u>control</u> are key themes of the play. How are they presented in these extracts?

<u>Prospero</u> is the centre of the play, not just the central character.

Sample answer with examiner's comments

Prospero rules the island with his magic. How does his *language* show how his use of power changes in the two extracts?

Essay 1 Band 2

Note: Many students stay in Band 2 because they make comments and pick out quotes but do not say **why** or **how** language is used in the extracts.

> Broad reference to how Prospero speaks but no explanation of what 'to point' shows about his use of power when speaking to Ariel.

> Choosing 'calls' and 'reminds' suggests some explanation of why Prospero speaks, but more exploration of the changes in tone of words is needed.

> Picks out the word 'slave' but should say more about what this shows about Prospero's power and how he treats his servants. He called Ariel 'malignant thing'. (Band 3 requires understanding of why words are chosen.)

In the first extract Prospero asks Ariel to describe the shipwreck. The way he speaks to Ariel is to say has he 'performed to point the tempest' Prospero thinks that he has his enemies caught so he calls Ariel 'brave spirit'. He does not like it when Ariel wants his freedom so he reminds him that he set him free when he was put in a pine tree by Sycorax. Prospero also calls Caliban a 'slave' because he tried to rape his daughter Miranda.

In extract 2 Prospero has all his enemies together but Ariel makes him feel sorry for Gonzalo. Prospero says he will release them, 'my charms I'll break'. When he gets out of his disguise the lords recognise him and he forgives them. He is pleased to see Gonzalo who helped him leave Milan, 'noble friend'.

At the end of the scene Prospero gives up his power and says he will 'drown' his book. Prospero gets his kingdom back and his daughter marries Ferdinand the son of the King of Naples.

> 'say' linked with the quotation does refer to language, but needs exploration.

> The quote is put in but needs to be linked to comment.

> Broad reference to what Prospero says needs to be developed further to gain higher marks.

Commentary

This essay would not reach a higher band, although the writer obviously knew the extracts and was aware of the play as a whole. Some comments are at the level of plot description, and whilst there is some explanation of how Prospero speaks, there is not enough exploration of the way language links to power. There is broad reference to what Prospero says, but not enough reference to why he says it. The quotations are relevant to points made but the language in them is not explored.

How to improve

Remember that both extracts **must** be dealt with as **equally** as possible.

Do not rush through telling the story. Take time to give your opinion on how words show Prospero's power. You may have some strong ideas on these. Does he speak to Caliban and Ariel with the same abusive tone? Does he enjoy challenging the gods and having the power to make graves open and to make roaring war? Discussion of the **effects** of language will give you band 4 or above.

Extract from an essay worthy of a higher band

As a master Prospero praises his servant Ariel when he carries out his orders 'to point'. He wants everything done exactly right so that his enemies will be in his power. He is so pleased with Ariel that he calls him 'brave spirit' but as soon as Ariel wants his freedom Prospero's language changes and becomes nasty: 'malignant thing'. This is a long word with hard 'g' sounds which makes Ariel out to be evil. Thing shows that he wants Ariel to think he is worthless.

On top of this he tortures Ariel's mind as he makes him re-live his imprisonment by Sycorax by describing how he was in a pine tree. His words become threatening as he says he will put him into an oak tree and make him suffer. Ironically his language shows that he is as bad as Sycorax. I think he is using his power badly.

Commentary

This paragraph shows awareness of language and some discussion, which puts it into Band 4. This is not too difficult if you use your own opinion about **how** language works.

Top 10 tips for the test

1. Make sure you are familiar with the layout and style of questions by looking at tests from previous years.
2. Read the question aloud in your head two or three times until you realise what it is really asking you to do.
3. Keep in mind performances of the play that you have seen in the theatre or on video, and remember what it was like acting out the set scenes with other people.
4. It is better to explore a few points in depth and discuss the effect of language in detail than to offer a series of general comments.
5. Don't ever just tell the story – answer the question.
6. Time spent on planning is time well spent. Practise doing a plan in five minutes so that in the real test you can create a plan within ten minutes.
7. Plan so that your main points are in a sensible order that responds to the question.
8. Provide evidence in quotations or refer to what happens and what is said to support your points. *(Remember not to waste time copying out long quotations but do make sure you comment on the effect of the language.)*
9. Make sure that your conclusion relates back to the question.
10. Leave time (but not too much!) at the end of the test to read through what you have written.

Planning your answer

Spend at least five minutes on planning in the test. The time available for this is limited, so it needs to be used well. The question is likely to be on one of the following:

- why characters behave as they do in the extracts given
- the impact of the language used in the extracts
- ideas, themes and issues that are relevant to the extracts
- how these extracts might be performed in the theatre.

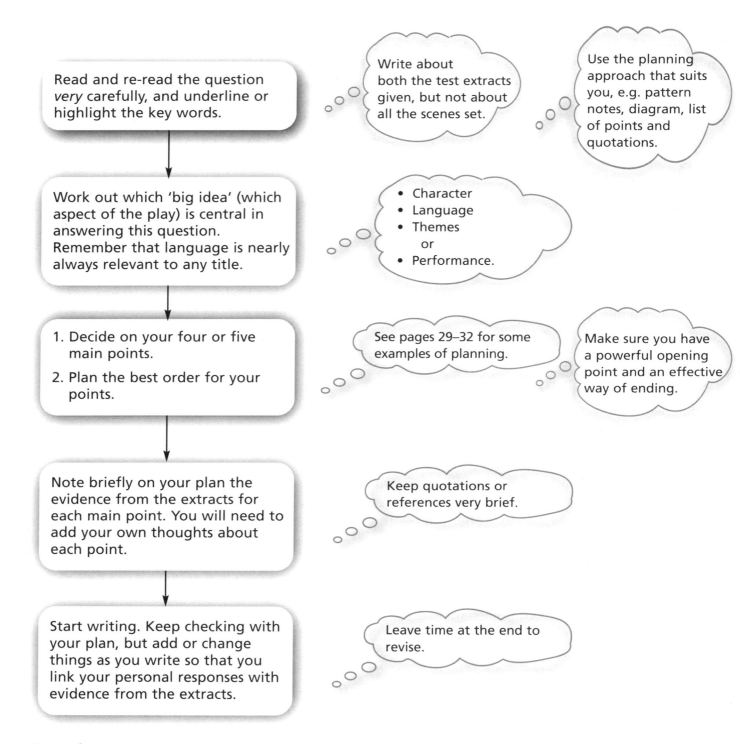

Read and re-read the question *very* carefully, and underline or highlight the key words.

Write about both the test extracts given, but not about all the scenes set.

Use the planning approach that suits you, e.g. pattern notes, diagram, list of points and quotations.

Work out which 'big idea' (which aspect of the play) is central in answering this question. Remember that language is nearly always relevant to any title.

- Character
- Language
- Themes
  or
- Performance.

1. Decide on your four or five main points.
2. Plan the best order for your points.

See pages 29–32 for some examples of planning.

Make sure you have a powerful opening point and an effective way of ending.

Note briefly on your plan the evidence from the extracts for each main point. You will need to add your own thoughts about each point.

Keep quotations or references very brief.

Start writing. Keep checking with your plan, but add or change things as you write so that you link your personal responses with evidence from the extracts.

Leave time at the end to revise.

Remember
Marking 300 similar answers does get boring, so examiners appreciate a personal voice in an answer that does not just state the obvious.

Planning a character answer

What do Extracts 1 and 2 show about Prospero's character?

The main points of a planned answer for this question are in bold. The bullet points underneath give more detail about the main ideas.

1. Introduction
- Prospero is a complex character with both good and bad qualities.
- He is the mastermind behind the events in the play and these are determined by his character.

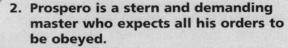

2. Prospero is a stern and demanding master who expects all his orders to be obeyed.
- Prospero has turned Caliban into a domestic servant who does all the menial jobs on the island – he refers to Caliban as his 'slave'.
- When Ariel reminds Prospero of his promise and asks for his freedom Prospero threatens to punish him: 'If thou more murmur'st, I will rend an oak, / And peg thee in his knotty entrails' (Act 1, Scene 2, lines 294–5).
- Prospero has planned the events very carefully and asks Ariel if he has 'Performed to point the tempest that I bade thee?' (Act 1, Scene 2, line 193)

3. Prospero can lose his temper quickly and when he is angry he can be vicious.
- Prospero begins Act 1, Scene 2 by calling Ariel 'my brave spirit', but when he is angry with him he calls him 'moody' and 'a malignant thing'.
- Prospero cannot forgive Caliban for his attack on Miranda and calls him a 'poisonous slave, got by the devil himself' (Act 1, Scene 2, line 320).
- When he meets his brother Antonio he calls him 'a wicked sir' and says that to call him brother 'would even infect my mouth' (Act 5, Scene 1, line 130).

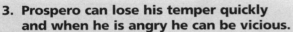

4. Prospero respects those who have helped him and has a strong sense of justice.
- Prospero calls Gonzalo his 'noble friend'.
- Prospero knows he will miss Ariel when he has been released but keeps his promise and says 'thou shalt have freedom'.
- Even though he forgives his brother and Sebastian for what they have done to him, he warns them that he is watching them for any future treachery and 'At this time / I will tell no tales' (Act 5, Scene 1, lines 126–8).

5. Prospero enjoys the power he has over the natural world and men.
- He controls Caliban, the son of a witch, who he keeps in service.
- He released Ariel from his prison and made him 'do me business in the veins o' the earth' (Act 1, Scene 2, line 255). When he casts away his magic he makes sure no one else can use it: 'I'll break my staff ... / I'll drown my book' (Act 5 Scene 1, lines 50–56).
- He can bring people back to life: 'Graves at my command / Have waked their sleepers, oped, and let 'em forth' (Act 5, Scene 1, lines 48–50).

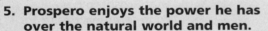

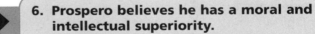

6. Prospero believes he has a moral and intellectual superiority.
- He believes that by forgiving the people who plotted against him he has 'nobler reason'.
- When he is satisfied that his punishment has worked on the conspirators, he releases them from the magic spell – 'the best comforter to an unsettled fancy cure thy brains' (Act 5, Scene 1, lines 58–9.

7. Conclusion
- Prospero needed to be ruthless, determined and use his magic powers in order to provide a husband for his daughter, regain his lost dukedom and make the conspirators regret their crimes against him.

Planning a theme answer

Number the four main points (in bold) in the order that you would put them in an answer.

We know that Prospero is the wronged Duke of Milan and learn that he did not just want death as revenge ('But are they, Ariel, safe?'). We also realise that he can exact any revenge, since he is in control of all that happens (Ariel: 'As thou bad'st me, / In troops I have dispersed them 'bout the isle').

Ariel: '... if you now beheld them, your affections / Would become tender ... Mine would, sir, were I human.' Ariel's reaction makes us focus on Prospero's humanity, or lack of it.

Prospero's violent anger with Ariel signals that Prospero is capable of rage: 'Thou liest, malignant thing!'

Prospero (to Antonio): 'I do forgive thee, / Unnatural though thou art!' Forgiving Antonio is a victory for Prospero.

Explain how words and actions from Extract 2 present ideas about vengeance and forgiveness. Illustrate by picking out words or phrases from the text.

Explain how certain words and actions in Extract 1 present ideas about vengeance and forgiveness. Illustrate by picking out words or phrases from the text.

Prospero: '... with my nobler reason 'gainst my fury / Do I take part.' Prospero knows that his greatest victory is over himself.

How far do these two extracts suggest that forgiveness is a greater victory for Prospero than vengeance?

Prospero: 'They being penitent, / The sole drift of my purpose doth extend / Not a frown further.' We recognise that Prospero has conquered his desire for revenge.

Explain why Prospero is central to the exploration of ideas about vengeance and forgiveness.

Give your personal response to the way ideas about vengeance and forgiveness are explored in both sections.

Prospero, like a playwright in some ways, is a magician who controls an imaginary world. We never really doubt his power over others, but wonder about his self-control.

If *The Tempest* had been just about gaining revenge, it would have been a tragedy that ended in bloodshed. As it is, the audience recognise that Prospero's forgiveness is the greater triumph.

In Extract 1, we see a powerful magician, full of anger, even with Ariel, who does his bidding. This anger is in part the result of his years of bitter exile and resentment.

In Extract 2, Prospero no longer needs his magic to control others – he needs to control his own emotions enough to realise that 'The rarer action is / in virtue than in vengeance'.

Planning a language answer

How is language used in the two extracts to show different aspects of Prospero's power?

Remember! Use **both** extracts equally.

Answer the question, which means referring to **power**.

Always comment on the quotes you use. Do not just put in a quote and expect the examiner to do the work.

The main points of a planned answer for this question are in bold. The points underneath give more detail about the main ideas.

Introduction
In both extracts Prospero enjoys his power.
- He enjoys Ariel's description of the storm with its violent imagery, 'flame' and 'burn', because he praises him.
- In Extract 2 he boasts that he has 'Set roaring war' and opened 'graves', but his greatest power is now power over himself.

EXTRACT 1

1. **Prospero is ruler of the island.** He is speaking to Ariel whom he has freed but now uses as a servant to make a storm to bring his enemies to him. At first he praises him, because he has obeyed 'to point' his orders. But when Ariel asks for freedom Prospero becomes nasty, calling him 'malignant thing'; 'thing' shows that he has no respect for Ariel, while 'malignant' sounds spiteful and unjust as Ariel is not evil.

2. **Prospero uses threatening language to make Ariel feel guilty for wanting his freedom.** He tortures Ariel as he makes him relive Sycorax's 'sorceries'. Ironically he says he will 'peg' him in an oak tree, the word 'peg' is harsh and shows how easily Prospero can hurt such a lovely spirit as Ariel.

3. **Prospero does not speak with respect to Ariel.** He makes Ariel feel guilty and ask for 'pardon'. He then gives his orders saying 'Go!' three times to emphasise his power. Caliban has tried to rape Miranda so Prospero treats him as a 'slave', but he seems to use the same language to both his servants.

EXTRACT 2

1. **Prospero has all his enemies in his power.** In his magic cloak he speaks like a magician with his 'charms' but his servant seems to have more mercy than Prospero. Ariel describes Gonzalo's tears which should make him 'tender'. Suddenly Prospero feels guilty that a spirit can have a 'touch a feeling'. His language changes as he begins to contrast 'virtue' and 'vengeance'. The alliteration emphasises his struggle between revenge and forgiveness.

2. **Prospero's long speech to the elves is like a spell** in which he describes the light 'printless' freedom which Ariel loves. His words describe the natural, free lives of the elves with verbs like 'chase' and 'fly', but in the middle of the speech he calls them 'weak'. Suddenly he remembers his power again when he says 'I'. He boasts that he is like a god. His language is wild and violent again: 'mutinous winds', 'roaring war', 'dread rattling thunder'.

3. **Prospero has all his enemies in a magic circle.** His words to Gonzalo are full of feeling – 'good' and 'loyal' – but he seems pleased that Sebastian is 'pinched' for his plot to kill his king as he says these words angrily. The pause shows his struggle as he knows Sebastian and Antonio are 'wicked'. Then he says 'I do forgive thee'. From this point there is a 'sea-change' Prospero enjoys the power of forgiveness.

Planning a performance answer

Number the four main points (in bold) in the order that you would put them in an answer.

When Ariel is describing the way he has performed all the magic actions, he should show his excitement and pride in his skill through his excited speech: 'in every cabin, / I flamed amazement.'

Ariel should show how angry he is with Prospero by speaking firmly and looking fierce: 'Is there more toil?'

Ariel should politely remind Prospero of his promise so he won't become angry: '... at which time, my lord, / You said our work should cease.'

When Ariel describes Gonzalo, he should speak to emphasise the sadness and use gestures to show Gonzalo's tears running off his beard: 'His tears run down his beard ...'

When he describes Ferdinand, Ariel should show his sympathy by folding his arms just like Ferdinand to emphasise the sad words 'and sitting, / His arms in this sad knot'.

After Prospero has criticised Ariel he should show his fear by speaking meekly: 'I will be correspondent to command ...'

Explain how your advice would encourage the actor to emphasise certain words or phrases in Extract 2.

Explain how your advice would encourage the actor to emphasise certain words or phrases in Extract 1.

If you were directing *The Tempest* what advice would you give to the actor playing Ariel on how to convey his different moods?

When Ariel knows he is about to be free ('Merrily, merrily shall I live now'), he should show his happiness in his lively movement and joyful singing.

Prospero: 'Yet with my nobler reason 'gainst my fury / Do I take part.' Prospero knows that his greatest victory is over himself.

Give examples of how Ariel's actions really help us to see what his mood is at a particular moment.

Comment on the overall impact of the performance on the audience.

When Prospero criticises Ariel, he should appear as small and unhappy as possible to show us how much Prospero's anger has upset him.

When Ariel knows he is really going to be free soon, he should appear very happy and lively to show his great relief that he will soon be free: 'I drink the air before me ...' He should rush off stage to do one of his final tasks.

By showing how angry he is with Prospero, then by emphasising how upset he is by the criticism, Ariel will make us sympathise with him against Prospero.

Ariel's performance is important when he shows that a non-human spirit can feel sympathy for Prospero's enemies because it helps the audience realise how powerfully the magic has affected them: 'Mine would, sir, were I human.'